EUREKA
CHRISTMAS RECITATIONS

Edited by

MATTIE B. SHANNON

Program Material For

Beginners ⚹ Primary ⚹ Junior
Departments

Also

Songs, Pageants, Pantomimes and Special Features
for Intermediates

ABINGDON PRESS
NASHVILLE

EUREKA CHRISTMAS RECITATIONS

Copyright 1939 The Stockton Press
Copyright renewal 1967
by Mattie B. Shannon

44th Printing 1989

No. 120853

MANUFACTURED BY THE PARTHENON PRESS
AT NASHVILLE, TENNESSEE, UNITED STATES OF AMERICA

Recitation
A GREETING
A greeting I would bring to you,
Although I am a tiny tot,
But if I speak out good and loud
I can welcome you as well as not!

* * *

Recitation
NO BETTER WAY
I've tried to do some thinking
To find a better way
To bring the greeting which we love
For blessed Christmas day;
But nothing else has come to me
'Cept "Merry Christmas";—so
I say with heart just filled with love
The greeting that you know;—
MERRY CHRISTMAS!

* * *

Motion Exercise
A SUGGESTION
(For two children.)

FIRST
We've[1] tried to make the program fine
That we now give[2] to you;
I'm sure[3] you must be thinking,[4] friends,
What each of you[5] might do.

SECOND
Perhaps you'll[6] get the idea which
We[7] think would be worth while;—
Just softly clap[8] your hands a bit
And smile,[9] smile, SMILE![10]

Motions. 1. Place the right hand on the breast. 2. Extend both hands outward toward the audience. 3. Speak very emphatically. 4. Nod the head. 5. Extend the right hand toward the audience and emphasize the word, "You." 6. Extend both hands toward the audience. 7. Place both hands on the breast and glance at the First Speaker. 8. Clap the hands softly. 9. Smile very broadly. 10. Both Speakers smile, bow and then exeunt, looking back over the shoulder at the audience and continuing to smile until they are out of view of the audience.

* * *

Recitation
SONG OF THE BELLS
Happy bells, so sweetly ringing,
Sound a word that all may hear,—
"Gladly welcome holy Christmas,
Praise the Lord in songs of cheer!"

* * *

Recitation
A PERFECT FRIEND
(For a small girl holding a large doll.)

My dolly is such a perfect friend;—
She's as kind as she can be;—
I hang her stocking to be filled
And she gives all the goodies to *me*!

Recitation
THIS IS THE TIME FOR GIVING
This is the time for giving
And joy we all may know
As we keep the birthday of our King
Who came to love us so.

* * *

Recitation
THERE IS LOVE
What shall I give to the dear little Stranger,
Whose home was a stable, Whose cradle a manger?
No treasure have I for He is a *King;*—
O yes, there is *love!* That is what I shall bring.

* * *

Exercise
A REQUEST
(For two children.)

FIRST
We've come to ask a favor, please;
We like this time of love and cheer;
Do you believe that we could have
Another one in half a year?

SECOND
It seems so hard to wait a year;—
The days and weeks are long, you know;
We'd like a *six months plan;*—Oh, please!
We're sure that you can make it so!

* * *

Exercise
SIZE DOES NOT COUNT
(For four Beginners.)

FIRST
We are quite small, as you can see;
SECOND
Oh, we are just Beginners!
THIRD
And yet we seem to do quite well;—
FOURTH
When it comes to *Christmas dinners!*

* * *

Recitation
THE FAVORITE
(For a boy who beats a small drum each time he repeats, "Ba-rum.")

I love a drum; I love its noise;
Ba-rum! Ba-rum! Ba-rum!
It seems to be just made for boys;—
Ba-rum! Ba-rum! Ba-rum!
Of course there's whistles you can blow
And songs to sing and greetings—
But none of these can stand a show
With just a little drum;—
Ba-rum! Ba-rum! Ba-rum!

Exercise
'TIS EVERYONE'S CHRISTMAS

(For three children.)

FIRST

'Tis *everyone's* Christmas
For dear Jesus came
To bless all the people,
To give all the same.

SECOND

But we are forgetting
This message so fair
And our Christmas blessings
Forgotten to share.

THIRD

'Tis *everyone's* Christmas:
Oh, we'll do our part
To bring joy and gladness
To some needy heart.

* * *

Motion Recitation
WHAT MOTHER HOPES

(For a small child who carries some toys in left arm, leaving the right one free for motions.)

I've got a great big smile[1] today;—
It spreads from ear[2] to ear[3];
Mother[4] hopes I'll keep this way
Throughout the whole,[5] long year.

Motions. 1. Smile. 2. With mouth spread wide, touch the right ear. 3. Holding the broad smile, touch the left ear. 4. Speak very emphatically. 5. Make a wide, sweeping motion with the right arm.

* * *

Exercise
WHO'LL ARRANGE IT?

(For four children.)

FIRST

I'd like to hear a broadcast
From dear old Santa Land;
If we could only tune it in,
I think it would be grand.

SECOND

We'd hear the little trumpets
As Santa tries them out;
We'd hear the little elves at work
With song and merry shout.

THIRD

There would be toy pianos;—
And think of all the drums!
They must be tested so they'll play
When Christmas time has come.

FOURTH

I'd like to hear a broadcast;
Oh, who'll arrange it, please?
I'd like to hear from Santa Land
Before dear Santa leaves.

Recitation
SPEAKING OF BOYS

(For a boy.)

There are some things not quite suitable
For boys to do, you know;—
They're not supposed to bake the cakes,
To embroider, knit or sew;
But—when the Christmas time is here
And dinner's ready,—Oh—
That's one thing at which any boy
Can surely make a go!

* * *

Recitation
PUZZLED

I go to school 'most every day
And study quite a bit
But this place called "Santa Land,"—
I wonder—where is it?

I've searched and searched with all my
   might
Within my geography book
But I can't find this "Santa Land,"
No matter where I look.

* * *

Exercise
HAPPY QUAKERS

(This exercise may be given by a group of small girls wearing Quaker bonnets.)

FIRST

Oh, we are happy Quakers
On blessed Christmas day;
Oh, we will testify to this
In truly Quaker way.

ALL (*nodding heads*)

Yea! Yea! Yea! Yea!

SECOND

Of course we'll not be selfish;—
We'll share our Christmas joys;
We will not think of self alone
Like naughty girls and boys.

ALL (*shaking heads negatively*)

Nay! Nay! Nay! Nay!

THIRD

We will remember Jesus
And celebrate His birth
By loving, serving, praising Him,
Who came to bless the earth.

ALL (*nodding heads*)

Yea! Yea! Yea! Yea!

FOURTH

Oh, has the truth we've given
Been lost to you, we say?
If not, then join us gladly
In saying,

ALL (*shaking heads negatively*)

Nay! Nay! Nay! Nay!

Exercise
A MERRY CHRISTMAS LINE

(For ten Beginners and a tall Junior. Each Beginner carries a pair of stockings which the Junior pins on the line after each recites. The committee should stretch a rope, covered with red and green crepe paper, across the back of the platform. This rope, with its gaily colored stockings, may form part of the platform decoration for the rest of the program.)

JUNIOR
Oh, this is a Christmas line, dear friend!
You shall see what we plan to do;
In a Christmas spirit that never ends,
We'll celebrate rightly, too.

FIRST BEGINNER
Oh, this is a *merry* Christmas line!

SECOND
What happens *indeed* you'll *see*:

THIRD
On it we'll hang some stockings fine;

FOURTH
They will fill childish hearts with glee.

FIFTH
They are not for us;—Oh, no, not one!

SIXTH
We hang them in bright, even row.

SEVENTH
Oh, we will have the greatest fun!

EIGHTH
We'll fill them from top to toe.

NINTH
After the program is finished tonight,
We'll cram them with presents fine!

TENTH
We'll give them away with great delight;—
That's a merry Christmas line!

* * *

Exercise
WITHIN A CIRCLE

(For two children who carry large wreaths of holly which they use as a "frame" for their smiling faces.)

FIRST
Within the circle of God's love
I live in happy way;
I know the Father up above
Will care for me each day.

SECOND
God's love will never know an end
And I will praise His name
Because His love encircles me
Just like a lovely frame.

Recitation before the Offering
CHRIST'S BIRTHDAY GIFT

We must have gifts for Christ the King
On this, His blest birthday;
We'll give to others in His name;—
That is the proper way;
So now we'll have to pause awhile
And ask, in this connection,
That, with thankful heart and happy smile,
You'll make a large collection!

* * *

Recitation
A SECRET

Christmas secrets are such fun!
I like them quite a lot
But sometimes they are hard to keep;—
And tell them you must not;
I said that I would never tell
'Bout Mother's gift;—it's *sweet*;
It comes within a pretty box
And it's *so good to eat!*

* * *

Recitation
UNDERNEATH THE MISTLETOE

When Daddy dear comes home at night
I'll hide behind the door,—and so
I'll jump out quickly! There I'll be—
Standing 'neath the mistletoe:

Of course I always get a kiss
But just at Christmas time, you know,
'Twill be more fun to have it there,—
Underneath the mistletoe.

* * *

Recitation
THE REASON IS QUITE CLEAR

A naughty boy is hard to find
When Christmas day is near;
They try to be polite and kind;—
The reason is quite clear.

* * *

Recitation
A HARD JOB FOR A MAN

Boys don't like to stand up here
But I'll do the best I can;
Speaking pieces just like this
Is hard to ask of any man;
And so I'll make it rather short,—
This Christmas speech of mine;
But Christmas wishes, kind and true,
Are packed in every line!

Exercise
A GRAND SECRET

(For six children. Each one carries the article he or she mentions.)

FIRST
Here's a lovely picture book!

SECOND
Here's a box of candy!

THIRD
Here's a doll that shuts its eyes!

FOURTH
Here's a drum that's dandy!

FIFTH
Here's a game that all would like;

SIXTH
Here's a ball that's new.

FIRST
And now we have a secret grand
To tell to all of you.

SECOND
The gifts that we have brought up here
For every one to see,

THIRD
Are going to some children small,—
As poor as they can be.

FOURTH
We'll put them by a Christmas tree,
All trimmed with balls that shine;

FIFTH
'Twill make those children happy, quite;

SIXTH
Don't you think that 'twill be *fine?*
* * *

Recitation
A CHRISTMAS TREE

A little fir grew in the midst of the wood;
Oh, there in his evergreen robe he stood!
His branches were sweet with the balsam
    smell,
His needles were green where the white
    snow fell,
And always contented and happy was
    he,—
The very best kind of a Christmas tree!
                    HENRY VAN DYKE.
* * *

Recitation
THE ANSWER

Santa Claus is sweet and jolly;—
We could be like him if we would;
Here's the answer to the secret;—
He works for others—doing good.

Recitation
SANTA'S MISTAKE

I found out something just today;—
Oh, it's quite true, I fear!
I wrote a letter, don't you know,
And made it very clear;
I asked dear Santa for a *bike*
That I could ride so far;
Well, I found out he *cannot read;*—
I got a *kiddie car!*

* * *

Exercise
BLESSED, BLESSED CHRISTMAS

(For eight Beginners.)

FIRST
This happy time all children love;—

ALL
'Tis blessed, blessed Christmas!

SECOND
We thank the Father up above,

ALL
For blessed, blessed Christmas!

THIRD
We know God sent us Jesus dear
To love and help all children here,
And so we praise with voices clear,

ALL
For blessed, blessed Christmas!

FOURTH
Many candles gleam tonight,

ALL
For blessed, blessed Christmas!

FIFTH
Sending out a message bright

ALL
For blessed, blessed Christmas!

SIXTH
Hearts with love are all aglow,
Songs are ringing here below,
Because the message we all know

ALL
Of blessed, blessed Christmas!

SEVENTH
Jesus came from heaven above
To live and help us with His love,

EIGHTH
And the angels from the sky
Sang, "Glory be to God on high!"

ALL
On blessed, blessed Christmas!

Finger Play Exercise
THE NAME WE LOVE

(For a group of Beginners, each of whom does the finger play action.)

FIRST

It takes five fingers—every one—
To spell a name we love,—
The name of God's dear Christmas Son
Who came from heaven above.

(As the name of "Jesus" is spelled out the children place the first finger of the right hand on thumb of the left hand on J. Touch the first finger of left hand on E, the second finger on S, the third finger on U and touch the little finger on S.

ALL IN UNISON

J - e - s - u - s—spells Jesus,—
Name so blest and dear;
We have learned to spell it right,
All we little children here.

* * *

Recitation
REAL HAPPINESS

I'm as happy as I can be
And I wish you all to hear it;
I'm thankful for the gift of Christ
And His love makes the Christmas spirit.

* * *

Exercise
LOVING PRAISE

(For a group of Beginners.)

FIRST

This is Jesus' birthday,
Whom the children love,
So we send our praises sweet
Up to heaven above.

(All sing the following lines to the familiar tune of "Happy Birthday to You.")

Loving Praises

Loving praises to you,
Loving praises to you,
Loving praises, dear Jesus,
Loving praises to you.

* * *

Recitation
SONGS OF PRAISE

Oh, angels were the first to sing
Songs of praises to our King;
We gladly sing our praise today
To keep His blest birthday.

Motion Recitation
OUR TASK

Angels[1] told the shepherds[2]
Of Christ[3] in stable dim,
And then the shepherds spread[4] the news
And gladly[5] told of Him;
Today the task is waiting
And we,[6] who love Him so,
Must tell of Jesus,[7] Prince of Peace,
Till all[8] the Saviour know.

Motions. 1. Look upward. 2. Look down and toward the left. 3. Right hand is extended toward the left. 4. Extend both hands far out to sides. 5. Smile very sweetly. 6. Place both hands on the breast. 7. Holding former position, look upward. 8. Both hands sweep out to sides.

* * *

Motion Exercise
WITHIN THE STORY

(For five Beginners.)

FIRST

A shining star[1] so clear and bright
Shone in the sky on Christmas night.

SECOND

And angels[2] sang a message true
That echoes all the wide[3] world through.

THIRD

A little Child[4] so sweet and fair
Was found within a stable[5] bare.

FOURTH

As shepherds and some Wise Men, too,
Came, bringing Him their worship[6] true.

FIFTH

Within this story we can find
The greatest Gift[7] to all[8] mankind.

Motions. 1. Extend right hand upward. 2. Look upward. 3. Extend both hands far out to sides. 4. Smile. 5. Extend right hand toward the right with gaze following. 6. Cross hands on the breast. 7. Repeat this very clearly. 8. Extend the hands outward in front and then sweep them out to sides.

* * *

Motion Recitation
CHRISTMAS COMES ARINGING

Christmas comes aringing[1]
With bells and happy songs
And voices[2] gladly singing;—
Joy[3] to this time belongs;
Christmas comes aknocking[4]
Upon your heart and mine;—
O gladly[5] we will welcome in
Our Saviour King[6] divine!

Motions. 1. Swing right hand as the first two lines are repeated. 2. Touch the lips lightly. 3. Smile broadly. 4. "Knock" against the breast with right fist. 5. Extend both hands in welcome. 6. Look up with an expression of great joy.

Exercise
LOVE GIFTS FOR JESUS

This exercise has been planned for two Primary Children and any number of Beginners. A rude manger should be placed at the center back of the platform and it should contain a lighted electric bulb or a large lighted flashlight.

The gifts which the children place within the manger should be practical ones;—either provisions to be distributed later or envelopes containing Christmas offerings.

(The two Primary Children enter the platform and take position at the center front.)

FIRST PRIMARY CHILD
I think the children long ago,
Who saw the Baby King,
Came softly to the manger low
And loving gifts did bring;
Perhaps a soft white cover
Or a tiny bird of clay
They brought and placed with loving
    hands
Beside His bed of hay.

SECOND PRIMARY CHILD
Oh, we may also bring him
Our thankful gifts of love
For if we give to others now
We give to Him above.

(As instrumental music is played the Beginners enter the platform carrying their gifts. The two Primaries lead them as they circle the platform, place their gifts within the manger and then form across the front of the platform. They all clasp their hands and bow their heads in an attitude of prayer as the Second Primary Child speaks.)

SECOND PRIMARY CHILD
Accept the gifts, dear Jesus,
We bring in Thy blest Name;
Oh, may we always live for Thee
And Thy great love proclaim.

ALL
Amen.

(Instrumental music is played as the Primary Children lead the Beginners from the platform.)

* * *

Motion Recitation
NOT SUITABLE

(For a small child carrying a toy dog.)

For my doggie[1] which I love
I'd[2] like to have a Christmas tree;
But what to use for trimming it
Quite badly puzzled[3] me;
The thing that he[4] would like the most
I couldn't use; Oh, no![5]
For *bones* would just look *terrible*[6]
On Christmas trees, you know!

Motions. 1. Pat the dog lovingly. 2. Speak very earnestly, looking directly at the audience. 3. Shake head sadly. 4. Hold the dog up for the audience to see. 5. Shake the head emphatically. 6. Frown.

Recitation
YOU'LL HAVE A PART

On this Christmas program you would
    like a part?
Why, of course, you may have it; bless
    your dear heart!
A part that is really and truly just
    great;—
You may have quite a part when they pass
    you the plate!

* * *

Motion Exercise
TREES AND FOLKS
FIRST
The very, very happiest trees[1]
In all the great wide[2] world today
Are the ones that stand with out-
    stretched[3] arms,
To give[4] their shining gifts away!
SECOND
The very, very happiest folks[5]
In all the great wide[2] world today
Are the ones who plan with loving hearts[6]
To share and give[7] in loving way.

Motions. 1. Look upward. 2. Extend both arms far out to the sides. 3. Extend the arms outward in front. 4. The arms sweep out to the sides; smile. 5. Extend right hand out toward the audience. 6. Place both hands on the heart. 7. Both hands are extended out in front with the palms up.

* * *

Recitation
NO JUSTICE THERE

You can get a map to show you how
To travel—well—just everywhere;
But I would ask you,—tell me now,
If this is right or just or fair;—
I've been trying most all day
And asking everyone around;—
Will some one please show me the way
To where dear Santa's house is found?

* * *

Exercise
ON FISHING

(For three children who hold a large net. A tennis net may be used.)

FIRST
Fishing is for summertime,—
That's what I'm sure you all would say,
But we've been fishing with a net
For merry Christmas day!
SECOND
We've "caught" some very lovely gifts;—
Some folks we'll not forget;
For Christmas gifts of every kind
Are here within this net.
THIRD
Oh, why not fish at Christmas time?
I'm sure it's very pleasant;
You do not need a hook and line;—
A net will catch a present!

Primary Selections

Exercise
MOTHERS ALWAYS DO

(For four girls each of whom carries the article
she mentions.)

FIRST

I made a gift for Granny;—
A little bag of blue;
Of course dear Mother helped me some;—
Mothers always do!

SECOND

I made a ball for Baby
Of wool so soft and new;
Oh, yes! Dear Mother wound it all;—
Mothers always do!

THIRD

I made my Dad some slippers;—
I crochet,—that is true,
But Mother made them fit the soles;—
Mothers always do!

FOURTH

I made dear Sis some candy
And it was lovely, too;
Of course my Mother showed me how;—
Mothers always do!

* * *

Recitation
A LEGEND

'Tis said that when the Christ Child lay
Within the manger bed of old,
A little fire burned briskly there
To keep away the chilling cold.

At early dawn a robin came
And hopped within the stable dim;
He saw the fire but feebly burned
And then—a lovely thought occurred to
    him;—
He beat his tiny wings until
The fire was clear and warm and bright
And lo, the feathers of his breast
Were crimson with the ruddy light!

Now, always, on his breast of red,
He wears the sign of service blest
Because he fanned the fire to warm
The Christ Who lay in infant rest.

* * *

Recitation
BETHLEHEM WILL COME TO ME

I'd like to go to Bethlehem
Where Jesus came to earth
And wander through the little town
So blessed by Jesus' birth,
But Mother told me—just tonight,
So sweet and lovingly,
That if I seek and worship Christ,
Bethlehem will come to me.

Recitation
A LESSON FOR SANTA

Santa Claus is sometimes queer
About the gifts he brings;—
He isn't always fair, I fear;—
I got so many things.
I saw a little girl today;—
Her doll of rags was made
And yet she seemed to think it grand;
'Twas all she had, I'm 'fraid.

Oh, all her clothes were ragged, too;—
I got a lovely dress,
A coat and hat and bright new shoes—
All kinds of toys, I guess;
I heard you speak then, Mother dear;
What did I hear you say?
You would be glad if I would like
To give some things away?

May I really, Mother dear?
O that would be just fine!
I'd love to share with that small girl
And see her blue eyes shine!
We'll choose the very nicest gifts
Among my lovely things;
We'll help dear Santa be more fair
About the gifts he brings.

* * *

Recitation
A REAL HELPER

(For a boy.)

Santa needs a hired man;—
That's true as true can be,
I wonder if he'd like to use
A fellow just like me?
I'd like to help him take the gifts
To children far and near;
Oh, well, I know how I *can* help;—
I'll *share* with children *here*.

* * *

Recitation
WE WELCOME YOU WITH
THANKFUL HEARTS

We welcome you with thankful hearts
At joyous, blessed Christmas time
And hope you've heard the message true
That bells and carols chime;
Jesus came to earth for us
That Christmas long ago
And now we keep His birthday here
Because we love Him so.

Exercise
A VERSE FOR CHRISTMAS
FIRST
We have a verse for Christmas dear;
We hope you'll think it very good;
We truly know it is quite clear;
We could accept it if we would.
SECOND
Now hear the words of Christ our Lord,
Who came to show us all the way;
Oh, we will earn His blest reward
If we use this verse on every day.
IN UNISON
"Inasmuch as ye have done it unto one
of the least of these my brethren, ye have
done it unto Me." Matthew 25:40.

* * *

Exercise
GLORY BE TO GOD
FIRST
A little manger bed for Jesus,
Perhaps some cattle standing by
While angels from the far-off heavens
Sang, "Glory be to God on High!"
SECOND
And now the world has paused to crown
    Him;
They bow before the holy King;
We are grateful for our Saviour;—
"Glory be to God," we sing.

* * *

Motion Recitation
A SUITABLE GIFT
(For a boy who has a baseball.)

I had a time[1] selecting
A gift for Mother dear[2]
But I have found the *very*[3] thing;—
Just see! I have it here;[4]
Sometimes, when Daddy isn't home;
She will pitch ball;[5]—you see?
And then, of course,[6] I know quite well,
Each day she'll[7] lend it to me.[8]

Motions. 1. Shake head sadly. 2. Smile. 3. Speak
very emphatically. 4. Hold the baseball up so the
audience can see it plainly. 5 Pass the ball from one
hand to the other. 6. Shake the head very emphatically. 7. Smile very broadly. 8. Hold the ball against
the breast.

* * *

Recitation
A SPLENDID IDEA
(For a small child carrying a large calendar.)

I have a splendid idea, I think;
Now hear me while I speak;
Let's make a brand new calendar
With a Christmas in every week!

Recitation
THE MEASURING VERSE
Every Christmas day I stand
Beside my play room door
And every time my Daddy finds
That I have grown some more,
He marks a tiny place to tell
How tall I am; and so,
I try to keep my body well
That I may grow and grow.

Daddy reads a verse to me,
On Jesus' birthday blest,
That I may see how Jesus grew
In every way that's best;
I understand it now quite well;—
I've said it every year
And I must try to grow just right
As Jesus did while here.

"Jesus increased in wisdom and stature,
and in favour with God and man." Luke
2:52.

* * *

Recitation
A LITTLE SOLOIST
I'm just a little soloist;
A carol I will sing
About the Baby Jesus blest,
Who came to be our King;
I love this song of Christmas;—
I feel 'twas meant for me,—
This precious hymn of Christ the Lord
And His nativity.

(The "Soloist" sings "Away in a Manger.")

* * *

Recitation
CHRISTMAS ARITHMETIC
There's a special kind of 'rithmetic
You do for Christmas day;
It isn't work;—it's just plain fun
If done in perfect way.

You add another stocking
Beside the mantel here
And leave a note quite plain to see
Addressed to Santa dear.

You ask dear Santa to subtract
Some things he's brought to you
And put them in the other hose
For some poor child;—Now do!

And then you'll *multiply* your joys
On happy Christmas day
And *add* to some one else's, too,
Subtracting in this way.

Exercise

THE STORY OF CHRISTMAS

(For six children.)

FIRST

A gleaming star shone in the evening sky
Long, long ago;
What did it see from its place on high,
Under its wondrous glow?

SECOND

Oh, there was a stable in Bethlehem
town,—
A holy place;
The star on that dwelling low looked down,
Lighting a Baby's face.

THIRD

Lo, shepherds were seen in the fields that
night,
Beside the fold,
And angels who winged through paths of
light,
Lifted eyes did behold.

FOURTH

The starry ray saw how the shepherds
went
With hurrying feet;
With worshipping hearts they lowly bent,
Gladly their Lord to greet.

FIFTH

And travellers were guided a long, long
way
To a King they sought,
And to the Child, Who in manger lay,
Wonderful gifts they brought.

SIXTH

The story is old but forever new
To faithful hearts
For sweetly it tells of a Saviour true,
Christmastide joy imparts.

* * *

Recitation

WE MUST WAKE TO HEAR THE MESSAGE

No one needs to call us loudly,
Waking us on Christmas day;
We are up quite bright and early;
Hurrying in happy way.
Have we wakened to the tidings
Of this very holy time?
We must wake to that great message;—
In the clearest notes 'twill chime.
There is need and grief and suffering,
Living in so many a heart;
We must waken to our duty
And do as best we can OUR PART.

Recitation

WE HAVE A BAND AT OUR HOUSE

We have a band at our house,—
Sweet music in the home,
But sometimes, just the notes you hear,
Would make you wish to roam;
Big Brother plays a flute quite well,—
At least it's good and loud;
Sister makes the accordion blast;—
You'd think it was a crowd;
The twins have each a large-sized
drum;—
They beat them with a will;
The Baby bangs the furniture
And hollers out until
You wonder just what quietness
Is like on Christmas day,
But then—we have a lot of fun
At our house, anyway!

* * *

Exercise

CHRISTMAS QUESTIONS

(For four Juniors.)

FIRST

Have we seen the little Christ Child
Legend says this night will roam?
He may be among the needy,—
A little child who seeks a home.

SECOND

Have we heard the angels singing
To the shepherds on the plain?
Open ears will hear the message
Ringing out in glad refrain.

THIRD

Have we seen the star of glory
That will lead us from on high?
If our souls by faith are lifted
We will find it in our sky.

FOURTH

Have we gifts that we may offer,
Worthy of a Saviour King?
There is no heart that can love Him
But a precious gift may bring.

FIRST

We will find the little Christ Child;

SECOND

We will hear angelic strain;

THIRD

The star of faith we'll find—clear-shin-
ing;

FOURTH

We'll give with loving hearts again.

Recitation
BABY JESUS, FAST ASLEEP

Baby Jesus, fast asleep,
In your little manger bed,
Where the shadows softly creep
And a star-ray crowns Thy head;
There are shepherds gathered round,
Worshipping by Thy small feet,
And Wise Men, on a journey bound,
Soon will come with treasures meet.

Baby Jesus, fast asleep,
Cradled with the humble kine,
Coming Shepherd of the sheep,
Lord and Saviour King divine,
May I worship Thee in truth,
Bringing Thee my heart's best love,
Pledged to serve Thee in my youth,
Gift of God from heaven above.

* * *

Exercise
CLEAR THE PATH FOR CHRISTMAS

(An exercise for three boys who wear out-door clothing and carry large shovels.)

FIRST
Clear the path for Christmas!
Oh, gladly work away!
We'll free the road of selfishness
For happy Christmas day!
SECOND
Clear the path for Christmas:
With hearts of love so true,
Oh, make a place for helpfulness
And good deeds we may do.
THIRD
Clear the path for Christmas
That we may find the way
To worship, love and praise the Lord
Who came on Christmas day.

* * *

Recitation
THE PROOF

(The boy who recites this should hold a report card.)

I've been studying quite hard at school;—
Been as good as I could be;
I thought I'd let dear Santa know
In a way that he could see;—
So when he comes to our house
And climbs down from the roof,
He'll find this card[1] addressed to him
Because it is a proof;—
It's my report card;—all my marks
Are written plain and clear;
Dear Santa'll say with pleasant smile,
"I must leave some fine gifts here!"

1. Hold the card up high.

Exercise
THE CHRISTMAS GIVERS

(This exercise should be planned for and made a real project in giving. Each speaker may lead a group of children who really bring gifts to be distributed later.

As instrumental music is played the children march on the platform.)

FIRST
We make a circle around the world;
Oh, Christmas givers are we!
We're only a few of the happy ones
Knowing joy that the world may see.

SECOND
The circle began in the long ago
When sages travelled so far
To bring their gifts to a Baby King
Whose followers today we are.

THIRD
The circle is large and it stretches now
Into every land on earth,
As rich and poor join hand in hand
To keep the Saviour's birth.

FOURTH
Though gifts are small that we may bring,
If love shall fill the heart,
We rightly give to the Saviour King;—
In this circle we have a part.

(The children circle the platform and leave their gifts at center back.)

* * *

Recitation
THE DREAM

I had such a dream on Christmas Eve.—
I'm glad it was not true;
I thought I saw old Santa Claus,—
His pack quite filled up, too;
But in my stocking, hanging there,
He put, why, not a thing!
Oh, even when I think of it
My eyes begin to sting!

But—when I waked on Christmas day,
I found my stocking there,
All filled with fruit and candies sweet;—
It was fine, I do declare!
But, when I think of children poor,
Who, just like in my dreams,
Will find their stockings empty quite,
Why, now, how sad it seems!

I think I'll share mine, don't you know;—
For at least one child it won't be so!

Acrostic Drill Exercise

CHRISTMAS STARS

(This may be made a beautiful and effective exercise. It requires fourteen children, each of whom carries a star-tipped wand or a large star made of pasteboard and covered with silver paper.

Each star is lettered with the letter which is used in the acrostic by the speaker.

As instrumental music is played the participants enter the platform. They circle the platform and take position in this way.)

CHRISTMAS

STARS

(The very smallest children are used for the line spelling "Stars.")

All bow.
All hold stars as high as possible.
Extend stars to the right.
Extend stars to the left.
Hold the stars in an even line and form in a straight line across the front of the platform.

FIRST

C Christmas stars are shining out
O'er all the world tonight,
Sending us blest messages
With their heavenly light.

SECOND

H Hope divine is given to men
Throughout the shadowed earth
If they receive the angel song
That rang at Jesus' birth.

THIRD

R "Remember," sang the Christmas stars,
"Just all the Saviour brings
And send your gratitude above
To crown the King of Kings."

FOURTH

I "In Jesus' name to those in need,
Give lovingly," they say,
"That all may know great happiness
Beneath our holy ray."

FIFTH

S "Send out the Christmas tidings now,"
The Christmas stars repeat,—
"Till all may seek the Saviour King
And worship at His feet."

SIXTH

T "To all the mighty Christ would bring
The blessing of His peace
That earth may live in brotherhood
And war and strife may cease."

SEVENTH

M Multitudes of stars now shine
Along the heavenly way
To tell us of the Bethlehem star,—
That bright and living ray.

EIGHTH

A   Along the years will ever glow
     The herald star divine
     So Christ will give His guiding light
     Within our hearts to shine.

NINTH

S   So we will look above and find
     In all its splendor bright
     The star of faith for us will gleam
     With holy, radiant light.

TENTH

S   Shine out, O stars of Christmas time,

ELEVENTH

T   To bring thy message blest,

TWELFTH

A   As joyous song and holy chime

THIRTEENTH

R   Remind us of our Guest.

FOURTEENTH

S   So we will pledge to Christ our all,

CHILDREN IN UNISON (*Holding stars high*)
    As far and wide thy glories fall.

(If possible the children should sing a selected song about Christmas stars before they circle the platform and exeunt.)

Motion Recitation

IT ISN'T WHAT YOU GET

At Christmas time it's fine[1] to have
A lot of gifts from far[2] and near
But Grandma knows the grandest[3] way
To have the best of Christmas cheer;—
She whispered[4] in my ear and said,
"No matter[5] where you chance to live,
It isn't what you *get*, my child;
You gather joy by what you *give*!"

Motions: 1. Smile. 2. Extend both hands outward at sides. 3. Clasp hands at the breast and smile. 4. Tilt the head and look up as though listening. 5. Give the rest of the verse very clowly, emphasizing the words in italic type.

Pageant

LOVE SHOWS THE WAY

(This is a very beautiful pageant and is quite effective. It may be given with but one rehearsal if the girl taking the part of Love will memorize her lines before the rehearsal.)

The committee may make the Golden Cord of Brotherhood with stripes of yellow or gold crepe paper plaited together. It should be of sufficient length to encircle the Group of the Nations gracefully. The number of girls required to carry it will depend upon the number of children used in the Group of Nations and the size of the platform.

As instrumental music is played ["O Come, All Ye Faithful" is appropriate.] Love, an Intermediate Girl in a long robe of soft pink, and having a name-band crossing her body diagonally from shoulder to waist, enters the platform, and stands at center, **not** at center front.)

LOVE

Oh, Love shows the way to Bethlehem,
Though nations may oft divide,
The Saviour is here to welcome them,
Where *Peace* reigns with *Joy* beside.

(Instrumental music is again played as Peace and Joy enter. Peace stands at the right and Joy at the left of Love. Peace wears a long robe of white and Joy a similar one of pale yellow.)

LOVE

Oh, truly I pray all may follow me,
Who bring you this earnest word;
Grateful for His nativity,
Oh, come ye and worship the Lord!

(As "O Come, All Ye Faithful" is sung, the children carrying the Flags of the Nations, come up the aisle, mount the platform and form in even number at right and left of the three symbolic figures. The children must not hide Love, Peace and Joy.

Love addresses the Group of the Nations.)

LOVE

The Saviour waits as once of old
He lay in humble Bethlehem;
Oh, all His glory may behold
As eyes of faith are given them:
He came as holy Prince of Peace;—
This was in the angels' song;
Oh, strife beneath His reign must cease
If hearts to Him belong.

(The Choir sings the first verse of "Hark! The Herald Angels Sing." Then, as instrumental music is played, a Group of Angels, carrying the Golden Cord of Brotherhood, come up the aisle and mount the platform. They should wear long, flowing robes of white. They pass the cord around the Children of the Nations with Love, Joy and Peace in the center, binding them together with the Golden Cord of Brotherhood. When the cord has been placed around the group the Children of the Nations kneel. They hold the tableau as the Choir sings the second verse of "Hark! The Herald Angels Sing.")

LOVE

The Golden Cord of Brotherhood,—
A gentle bond and sweet,
Will bind the nations for their good
Who kneel at Jesus' feet.

(The Children of the Nations rise. As the Choir sings the last verse of "Hark! The Herald Angels Sing," the Angels lead the recessional from the platform, followed by Love, Joy and Peace walking together and then the Children of the Nations, marching two by two.)

THE END

Junior Selections

Exercise

A KETTLE OF GIFTS

(This exercise is planned for a group of Camp Fire Girls who may be in costume.

A camp fire may be suggested by having a lighted electric bulb or a large lighted flashlight covered with red and orange paper and then fagots placed over this.

A large kettle is hung on a tripod over the "fire." The gifts which the girls put in the kettle should be practical ones;—gifts of groceries or fruit which may be given to a needy family after the program. The exercise should not be given just for entertainment.

The girls may enter the platform singing a selected song. Several songs are found at the end of this book. The girls seat themselves around the fire and finish the song. Each girl rises as she speaks and then places her gift in the kettle.)

FIRST SPEAKER

We've built a fire of kindness
And this is what we'll brew,—
A mixture filled with kindly gifts,
Of thoughts of service true.

SECOND

We wish to share our blessings
So we will place in here
Some gifts for others in the name
Of Christ, our Saviour dear.

THIRD

We know some folks are hungry,—
Some pantry shelves are bare;
We'll put some gladness in their hearts
By putting food up there!

FOURTH

We wish this kettle to be filled
Right to the very brim
So other folks who love the Christ
May help us serve for Him.

FIFTH

Our deeds will speak of Jesus
And that is just our plan;
We'll also place good wishes here
With package and with can.

SIXTH

We wish to send out gladness
On happy Christmas day;
We really think we'll help a bit
By doing just this way!

SEVENTH

And so we'll share with others
With such a happy will
And find that gladness comes to us
As we this kettle fill!

EIGHTH

If you should wish to join us,
There's room for more, you see!
Just bring your gifts and place them
here;—
How pleased some folks will be!

The girls sing again as they exeunt.

Exercise

THE SAVIOUR IS HERE

(The exercise is planned for a group of Juniors, three of whom are speakers. As instrumental music of "There's a Song in the Air" is played the group enters the platform, followed by the speakers. The speakers stand in front of the group.)

FIRST SPEAKER

A beautiful song in the hush of the night
Rings out over Bethlehem plain
And a message of joy from angels of light
Is heard in that heavenly strain.

SECOND

A wonderful star is a beacon divine
For it leads searching wise men to Christ
And there, 'neath the star that forever
    will shine,
They give Him their treasures unpriced.

THIRD

A soft little cry in a sweet Infant voice
Is heard by a mother's keen ear,
And lo, all the world must hear and rejoice
For the Saviour of mankind is here!

(The group sings the first verse of "There's a Song in the Air." This may be found in many hymnals and books of sacred or Christmas songs.)

"There's a song in the air,
There's a star in the sky;
There's a mother's deep prayer
And a Baby's low cry.
And the star rains its fire
While the beautiful sing
For the manger of Bethlehem
Cradles a King."

* * *

Recitation

A GUIDING STAR

A star once guided travellers on
To where the Christ was found
And there, before a manger low,
They gladly gathered round.

Oh, I may be a star so bright
And guide with shining ray
If I but say with smiling face,
"Come to Bible School today!"

* * *

Recitation

YOU MAY GET ABOARD

(For a small boy carrying a toy ship.)

The Christmas ship quite soon will sail;—
With joy and sweetness it is stored;
If you will share your blessings, friends,
Why come—and you may get aboard!

Recitation
THE CHRISTMAS LIST

My Christmas list is finished now
And each gift has been bought;
I did not have so much to spend
To get the things I sought;
But every one will have a gift;—
All those I love so well;
They may be valueless or small
But of great love they'll tell.

And one Name always heads the list;—
Ah, yes, beyond a doubt,
The Christ must come the first of all;—
How sad to leave Him out!
Of earthly friends and loved ones all,
He stands above the rest;—
It is His birthday we must keep,—
Our Lord and Saviour blest.

With this one gift I say these words,
"Inasmuch as ye
Will give unto the least of these,—
Ye give it unto *Me*."

* * *

Recitation
THE VERY LOVELY STORY

There's a very lovely story
From the old Judean hills;
We can ne'er forget its glory
And its beauty and its thrills.

When we share its love and blessing—
All its news, so true and dear,—
Greater joy we are possessing
That will last throughout the year.

* * *

Recitation
A GIVER

They had no gifts from Christ the Lord;—
They came to give, instead;
They gladly placed their treasures rare
Around His manger bed;
They did not know His power to heal
The sinsick and the weak;
They did not hear the loving voice
Of Him they came to seek.

Ah, well I know His power divine,—
The greatness of His love;
His guiding voice can speak to me
And lead my thoughts above;
Oh, shall I only *take* the gifts
That come, divinely blest?
No; I must be a *giver*, too,
And offer Him my best.

Exercise
LIGHTS ALONG THE ROAD

(An exercise for an Intermediate and five Juniors. If desired they may be costumed but the exercise will be effective without special costuming. The Intermediate may wear a long robe of yellow and the Juniors may have similar ones of white. The Juniors may have name-bands. Five large candles should be arranged across the back of the platform, forming part of the platform decoration. The Intermediate carries a large lighted candle with which she lights one of the candles after each Junior recites.

As instrumental music is played the Intermediate enters the platform followed by the Juniors, the Intermediate taking position in front of the Juniors as she speaks and then moving aside to light the candles as the Juniors repeat their verses.)

INTERMEDIATE

There are lights along the road that lead
To Christmas day so blest and bright
And those who truly seek the way
Will find a blessed path of light.

FIRST JUNIOR

We know that *Love* came down to earth
At Christmas time of old
For Jesus was God's Gift of Love,
Of Whom the prophets told.

SECOND

O *Faith* forever shines more clear
Since Jesus' holy birth
As God filled the promise made
Of a King for all the earth.

THIRD

So *Hope* will also light the way
That leads men to the Christ
For through His love He gives to all
Rich blessings—yet unpriced.

FOURTH

A *Joy* the world can never give
Is won through Christ the King;—
"Good tidings of great joy for all,"
We hear the angels sing.

FIFTH

The Saviour longs to give His *Peace*
To nations—one and all;
Oh, they must find the way to Him,
Before Him humbly fall.

INTERMEDIATE

(*after all candles are lighted*)
There are lights along the road
That lead all men to Him;
Their radiant gleam shall never pale,
Their glory shall not dim.

(Instrumental music is played as the Intermediate leads the Juniors from the platform.)

Musical Exercise

CHRISTMAS

(This exercise is arranged for eight Juniors from the beautiful and well-known poem by Phoebe Carey.

As instrumental music of "Joy to the World" is played the Juniors enter the platform and take position at center.

They sing "Joy to the World" or other selected carols.)

FIRST

This happy day, whose risen sun
Shall set not through eternity,
Is holy day when Christ the Lord
Took on Him our humanity.

SECOND

For little children everywhere
A joyous season still we make;
We bring our precious gifts to them,
Even for the dear Child Jesus' sake.

THIRD

Thou blessed Babe of Bethlehem,
Whose life we love, whose name we laud,
Art Brother through Whose poverty
We have become the sons of God.

FOURTH

We do remember how, through Thee,
The sick were healed, the halting led,
How Thou didst take the little ones
And pour Thy blessings on their head.

FIFTH

And Lord, if to the sick and poor,
We go with generous hearts today,
Or kindly serve the needy ones,
We follow in Thy blessed way.

SIXTH

O wilt Thou not, in wondrous grace,
And for Thy tender charity,
Accept the good we do to these
As we had done it unto Thee?

SEVENTH

If any act that we can do,
If any thought of ours is right,
O grant the prayer we lift to Thee
May find acceptance in Thy sight.

EIGHTH

Hear us and give to us today,
In answer to our earnest cries,
Some portion of that sacred love
That drew Thee to us from the skies.

ALL IN UNISON

Amen.

(The Group may sing, "'Tis Love Makes Our Christmas So Dear." This song is found on page 31.)

Drill Exercise

WE TRAVEL UNTO BETHLEHEM

(For a group of Juniors. The Leader carries a Conquest Flag. The others may carry flags of the Nations.

As some good march music is played the Juniors march on the platform carrying the flags over their right shoulders. They circle the platform twice and then take position across the front with the Leader standing at the center of the group.)

LEADER

We travel unto Bethlehem,
The children[1] of the world,
Beneath a banner bright and fair,
The Conquest Flag,[2] unfurled;
We should unite[3] in brotherhood
With Christmas skies above
And claim our Lord[4] as "Prince of Peace,"
The Christ Child Whom we love.

1. All hold the flags up high. 2. The Leader waves the Conquest Flag. 3. All hold the flags so that they touch. 4. Place the flags across breasts and look upward.

LEADER

Beneath the banner[5] of our Lord
We pledge[6] to live aright.
In peace and love and charity,
And serve with spirits bright;
We travel unto Bethlehem
Again to find our King
And, as we bow in worship true,
Our pledge to Him we'll bring.[7]

5. The Leader holds the Conquest Flag up high. 6 All place left hands on hearts and look at flags they hold, and then up at the Conquest Flag. 7. As instrumental music is played they circle the platform and exeunt.

* * *

Recitation

LET US KEEP CHRISTMAS

No matter what happens of sorrow or pain,
Let us keep Christmas with faith once again;
Whatever befall us of doubt, grief or fear,
O may we see angels when Christmas is here!
Angels of joy that sing forth from the sky
To tell us the Saviour of mankind is nigh.

Though the shelter now left us is humble and low,
We'll think how the Christ Child once came, long ago,
And a candle may shine through a window tonight,
To tell of a faith that is starry and bright;
Oh, we will keep Christmas with hope strong and sure
For its messages blest through the ages endure.

Pageant Exercise

HEART GIFTS

CHARACTERS

DOLLY—A small girl, poorly dressed in modern clothes.

MOTHER—Also poorly dressed in modern clothes.

LOVE
JOY
OBEDIENCE } Juniors who may wear long robes of white or of the
TRUTH   pastel shades, made of cheesecloth or other soft material.
SERVICE
GRATITUDE

The part of Dolly should be given to a child who is small for her age and who can handle the lines with expression.

A committee should have ready six stars of tinsel or silver paper of a suitable size for decorating a small evergreen tree. The tree should stand on a table at the center of the platform and should be untrimmed at the beginning of the playlet.

The scene should suggest a poorly furnished living room. A large easy chair should stand at the right front. This chair should hold several cushions and have a shawl draped over its back.

(*Dolly enters and stands, looking at the tree, her face smiling and happy.*)

Dolly—Dear little Christmas tree! You are very pretty even if you have no shining ornaments. You are pretty just as you are. Of course, I do like balls and stars and tinsel—but Mother said the ornaments we used to have were burned in the fire that took away our home and—there is no money this year to buy any more. But oh, I *do* love you just as you are!

(*She moves to the chair at right front and is seated. She sighs deeply.*)

I know that—somehow or other—Mother will have a Christmas gift for me tomorrow. I have nothing to give her and it makes me sad. She will come home very tired tonight. Christmas time is such a busy time in the store where she works. I tried to fix everything for our supper—and now I am tired, too.

(*She yawns, sighs, settles back among the cushions and closes her eyes. She seems to sleep. Soft music is played for a moment.*)

The Mother appears at the left entrance and peeps in. She smiles, seeing Dolly asleep and enters very quietly. She carries six silver or tinsel stars. She moves to the tree and quietly places the stars there. She hangs them so that they all show and steps back a moment to see the effect. Then she takes the shawl from the back of the chair, places it over Dolly and quietly exits.

Music is played as Love, Joy, Obedience, Truth, Service and Gratitude enter. They stand in a semi-circle around Dolly.)

Love (*calling softly*)—Dolly! Dolly!

(*Dolly stirs, yawns and opens her eyes slowly.*)

Dolly—Oh! Oh!

(*She sits upright and rubs her eyes.*)

Love (*smiling*)—We have come to see you this Christmas Eve, Dolly.

Dolly—You look so bright and pretty. Why did you come—but of *course* I am glad to see you!

Love—We came because we heard you say you had no gift for your Mother on Christmas—but see! On your tree hangs stars which are precious gifts you may give your Mother tomorrow.

Dolly (*looking at the tree*)—Oh, what beautiful stars! But I don't understand what you can mean.

(*Love goes to the tree and touches one of the stars.*)

Love—This is Love. This is a beautiful gift which you have for your Mother. It is more precious than gold or silver or shining gems and your Mother will receive it with a very thankful heart.

(*Joy moves to the tree and touches a star.*)

Joy—And here, dear child, is the gift of Joy. Your little smiling face, your happy songs, are very valuable and mean much in your Mother's life. Be always ready to give her this shining gift.

Obedience (*touching a star*)—And here is a gift which every parent appreciates—Obedience. No child who gives this need say she had no gift. Your Mother has a right to expect this treasure and beautifully you give it to her.

Truth (*as she touches a star*)—Here is the gleaming star of Truth. Your Mother is not always with you and many times it would be easy to tell her a falsehood, but you try to give her this lovely gift which is always precious.

Service (*her fingers on a star*)—My dear little girl, the love in your heart leads you to do little deeds of helpfulness each day and thus may give your Mother the sweet gift of Service.

Gratitude (*smiling brightly as she touches the last star*)—Gratitude is a gift which everybody would like to own. You have this to give your Mother. You are grateful for what you have received and do not envy others. That is true Gratitude.

Dolly—Oh, thank you for telling me this! My Christmas day will be a happy one because I know I do have something to give my dear Mother.

(*As soft music is played the symbolic characters quietly exeunt. Dolly cuddles down in the chair and again resumes the appearance of slumber. Mother enters from the left and crosses to Dolly. She smooths Dolly's hair and touches her gently, waking her. Dolly stirs, opens her eyes and raises her arms to her Mother.*)

Dolly—Oh, Mother! I didn't know you were home.

Mother—Come, dear, supper is ready. You were sweet to have everything fixed for me.

Dolly (*remembering her dream*)—Oh! (*She turns and looks at the tree.*) The stars are really there! It's just as I dreamed.

Mother—You were dreaming, dear?

Dolly (*slowly*)—I must have been. I was sad because I had no Christmas gift for you—then I fell asleep. I thought that Love, Joy, Truth, Obedience, Service and Gratitude came. They hung stars on my tree and told me they were my gifts to you—Love—Joy—Truth—Obedience—Service and Gratitude.

Mother (*tenderly*)—And so you do give me those gifts, dear child, not only on Christmas but every day. That is real heart giving. Come, dear, let us have our supper and you shall tell me about your dream.

(*Mother and Dolly exeunt as the music increases in volume.*)

Special Features

Feature Exercise

RING OUT THE CHRISTMAS MESSAGE

(This exercise has been arranged from "A Christmas Hymn" by Eugene Field and it requires a Group of Juniors, a Group of Intermediates, a Group of Primaries and two Intermediate Speakers.

As instrumental music is played the two Speakers enter the platform. The First Speaker stands at the extreme right front and the Second Speaker at the extreme left front. When they are in position the Juniors enter the platform singing "HEAR THE CHRISTMAS BELLS." This song may be found on page 30.)

Song by Juniors

HEAR THE CHRISTMAS BELLS

(When they have finished the song the Juniors form in back of the First Speaker.)

FIRST SPEAKER

"Sing, Christmas bells!
  Say to the earth this is the morn
Whereon our Saviour King was born;
  Sing to all men—the bond, the free,
The rich, the poor, the high, the low,
  The little child that sports in glee,
The aged folk that tottering go,—
  Proclaim the morn
  That Christ is born,
That saveth them and saveth me!"

(The Group of Intermediates enter the platform and take position at the center. They sing the first and third verses of "Hark! The Herald Angels Sing." These words may be found on page 26 and the carol is included in most hymnals.)

Song by Intermediates

HARK! THE HERALD ANGELS SING

(After their song the Intermediates form in back of the Second Speaker.)

SECOND SPEAKER

"Sing, angel host!
  Sing of the stars that God has placed
Above the manger in the east.
  Sing of the glories of the night,
The Virgin's sweet humility,
  The Babe with kingly robes bedight,—
Sing to all men where'er they be
  This Christmas morn
  For Christ is born,
That saveth them and saveth me."

(The Primaries enter the platform and stand in the center. They sing the following verses of "Away in a Manger.")

Song by Primaries

AWAY IN A MANGER

"Away in a manger, no crib for a bed,
The little Lord Jesus lay down His sweet head.
The stars in the sky looked down where He lay,
The little Lord Jesus asleep on the hay.

Be near me, Lord Jesus, I ask Thee to stay,
Close by me forever, and love me, I pray.
Bless all the dear children in Thy tender care,
And fit us for heaven to live with Thee there."

FIRST SPEAKER

Ring out the Christmas message sweet
Till men may hear, where'er they be;
    O praise the morn!
      The Christ is born,
That saveth them and saveth me!

SECOND SPEAKER

Ring out the Christmas message sweet
Till echoes sound both far and near;
    O praise His name,—
      Through love Christ came;—
'Tis love that makes our Christmas dear!

(A solo voice sings the verses of " 'Tis Love Makes Our Christmas So Dear." This song may be found on page 31. All participants on the platform join in singing the chorus and then they march from the platform, led by the two Speakers, as instrumental music is played.)

Recitation

A HYMN OF PEACE

Angel of Peace, thou hast wandered so
    long!
Spread thy white wings to the sunshine
    of love!
Come while our voices are blended in
    song,—
Fly to our ark like the storm-beaten dove;
Speed o'er the far-sounding billows of
    song,
Crowned with thine olive-leaf garland of
    love—
Angel of Peace, thou hast waited too long!

Brothers we meet, on this altar of thine,
Mingling with gifts we have gathered for
    thee,
Sweet with the odors of myrtle and pine,

Breeze of the prairies and breath of the
    sea!
Meadow and fountain and forest and sea!
Sweet is the fragrance of myrtle and pine,
Sweeter the incense we offer to thee,
Brothers once more round this altar of
    thine!

Angels of Bethlehem, answer the strain!
Hark! a new birth-song is filling the sky!
Loud as the storm-wind that tumbles the
    main,
Bid the full breath of the organ replay,
Let the loud tempest of voices reply,
Roll its long surge like the earth-shaking
    main!
Swell the vast song till it mounts to the
    sky,—
Angels of Bethlehem, echo the strain!

                OLIVER WENDELL HOLMES.

Pantomime Musical Number

THE CHRISTMAS SONGS

(As instrumental music is played four girls, costumed in long, flowing robes, of white or pastel shades, enter and take position on the platform, standing in this way.)

— —

— —

FIRST GIRL

"And there were in the same country shepherds, abiding in the field, keeping watch over their flock by night.

And lo, the angel of the Lord came upon them, and the glory of the Lord shone round about them: and they were sore afraid.

And the angel said unto them, Fear not: for, behold, I bring you good tidings of great joy, which shall be to all people.

For unto you is born this day in the city of David a Saviour, which is Christ the Lord.

And this shall be a sign unto you; Ye shall find the babe wrapped in swaddling clothes, lying in a manger.

And suddenly there was with the angel a multitude of the heavenly host praising God, and saying,

Glory to God in the highest, and on earth peace, good will toward men." (Luke 2:8-14.)

(A Concealed Chorus sings the first verse of "Hark! The Herald Angels Sing.")

"Hark! The herald angels sing,
'Glory to the new born King;
Peace on earth, and mercy mild;
God and sinners reconciled.'
Joyful, all ye nations, rise,
Join the triumph of the skies;
With the angelic host proclaim,
Christ is born in Bethlehem.
    Hark! The herald angels sing,
    'Glory to the new-born King.' "

SECOND GIRL

"Unto us a child is born, unto us a son is given: and the government shall be upon his shoulder; and his name shall be called Wonderful, Counsellor, The Mighty God, The Everlasting Father, The Prince of Peace." (Isaiah 9:6.)

(The Concealed Chorus sings the third verse of "Hark! The Herald Angels Sing.")

"Hail the heaven-born Prince of Peace
Hail the Sun of righteousness!
Light and life to all He brings,
Risen with healing in His wings.
Mild He lays His glory by,
Born that men no more may die,
Born to raise the sons of earth
Born to give them second birth.
    Hark! The herald angels sing,
    'Glory to the new-born King.' "

THIRD GIRL

"O sing unto the Lord a new song: sing unto the Lord, all the earth. Sing unto the Lord, bless His name; show forth His salvation from day to day.

Declare His glory among the heathen, His wonders among all people." (Psalm 96:1-3.)

(The Concealed Chorus sings the first verse of "Joy to the World.")

"Joy to the world! the Lord is come:
Let earth receive her king;
Let every heart prepare Him room
And heaven and nature sing."

FOURTH GIRL

"O Zion, that bringeth good tidings, get thee up into the high mountain; O Jerusalem, that bringeth good tidings, lift up thy voice with strength; lift it up, be not afraid; say unto the cities of Judah, Behold your God!" (Isaiah 40:9.)

(The Concealed Chorus sings the second verse of "Joy to the World.")

"Joy to the world! the Saviour reigns;
Let men their songs employ;
While fields and floods, rocks, hills and plains,
Repeat the sounding joy."

(As instrumental music is played a fifth Girl enters and takes position at the center front. Her costume is similar to that worn by the others. She recites while all give the pantomimic action.)

FIFTH GIRL

Far over[1] the star-lit night there rang
Music from angel[2] choir;
White-robed angels[3] from heaven sang
To shepherds[4] by low watch-fire;
The fire gleams[5] died 'neath a mystic light
That flooded the hill[6] and plain,[7]
For lo, a Saviour[8] was born that night,
Proclaimed[9] by a living strain.

1. The right hand moves up and to left, then sweeps across to the right, with gaze following. 2. Hands return to sides, gaze remains as before and head is tilted as though listening. 3. Both hands move upward. 4. Both hands sweep down and out to sides. 5. Look down and toward the right. 6. Both hands move outward at shoulder height. 7. Both hands, extended outward, move down to sides. 8. The hands meet at the breast. 9. Hold former position: expression of great joy.

(The Choir sings the first verse of "It Came Upon the Midnight Clear.")

"It came upon the midnight clear,
That glorious song of old,
From angels bending near the earth
To touch their harps of gold:
'Peace on the earth, good will to men,
From heaven's all gracious King.'
The world in solemn stillness lay
To hear the angels sing."

FIFTH GIRL

Far[10] over the path of earth it rings,—
Time[11] cannot dim the notes;—
To tell the coming of King[12] of Kings,
The anthem forever floats;
And songs awaken in saddened[13] hearts
That travel[14] to Bethlehem,
Receiving the peace[15] the Christ[16] imparts
With the hope[17] that awaits for them.

10. Both hands sweep far out to sides. 11. Hands are clasped at waist line. 12. The right hand sweeps upward oblique. 13. Both hands are placed over the heart. 14. Right hand moves out to side with gaze following. 15. Left hand is placed on the breast. 16. The left hand remains on the breast as the right hand is extended upward. 17. Both hands meet at breast; smile tenderly.

(The Choir sings the second verse of "It Came Upon the Midnight Clear.")

"Still through the cloven skies they come,
With peaceful wings unfurled,
And still their heavenly music floats
O'er all the weary world:
Look now! for glad and golden hours
Come swiftly on the wing:
O rest beside the weary road
And hear the angels sing."

(As instrumental music is played the girls exeunt.)

Recitation

THE LEGEND OF THE TOPAZ

There is a legend that forever brings
A story of the Wise—the eastern kings;
One of these a topaz brought the Christ,—
An Ethiopian topaz with a worth unpriced;
All men were envious; they'd possess this gem,
Worthy to be placed in royal diadem;
For this rare jewel held magic, so 'twas said
And lo, 'twas placed beside a lowly bed!

And now the Christ Child walks the shadowed earth
At Christmas time, when men would keep His birth,
The gleaming topaz held within His hand,
And those who give Him shelter through the land,
Receive a power,—a great, transforming power
Which is the gift of Christ at this bright festal hour;
How sweet the truth within this legend brief!—
A welcomed Christ brings power;—'tis our belief!

Recitation

THE MOTHER-HEART

"And all they that heard it wondered at those things which were told them by the shepherds.

But Mary kept all these things and pondered them in her heart." (Luke 2:18-19.)

The Mother held the Child so fair,—
God-given to her keeping,
While angel song rang through the air
And lulled the Babe to sleeping.
Wide-eyed shepherds softly came
And bowed before the manger.
Kings of earth, 'neath starry flame,
Were led to Infant Stranger.
Rich gifts were placed beside His bed,—
Gold, frankincense and myrrh;
She pondered;—kissed the tiny head
And sad the heart of her.

Pantomime Exercise

THE SKY CAN STILL REMEMBER

(This beautiful and well-loved poem by Phillips Brooks has been arranged as a pantomime number for three Intermediates. When possible they should wear long robes of soft material, loosely belted at the waist. One of the familiar Christmas carols, played softly, should serve as an introduction.)

FIRST

The sky[1] can still remember
The earliest Christmas[2] morn,
When in[3] the cold December
The Saviour[4] Christ was born.
No star[5] unfolds its glory,
No trumpet[6] wind is blown,
But tells the Christmas story[7]
In music[8] of its own.

1. Both hands are extended upward and far out to sides; gaze is directed upward. 2. Look directly at the audience and smile tenderly. 3. Both hands sweep out to sides at shoulder height. 4. Right hand moves slowly down to waist height, left returns to side; gaze is directed toward the right. 5. Right hand is extended upward oblique. 6. Hands are clasped at the waist line and head is tilted as though listening. 7. Hands sweep out to sides. 8. Hands are clasped at the breast.

SECOND

O never-failing[9] splendor:
O never-silent[10] song
Still keep the green[11] earth tender,
Still keep the gray[12] earth strong,
Still keep the brave earth[13] dreaming
Of deeds[14] that shall be done,
While children's[15] lives come streaming
Like sun-beams[16] from the sun.

9. Both hands are extended outward at shoulder height, eyes directed upward; expression of joy. 10. The hands are clasped at the breast, gaze directed as before and expression the same. 11. The right hand moves down with gaze following. 12. The left hand moves down as gaze is directed in that direction. 13. Both hands are extended at the sides and gaze is directed downward. 14. Hold former position as voice increases in power. 15. Right hand is extended toward the right, left hand is placed on the breast; expression of joy and tenderness. 16. Holding former position, look upward.

THIRD

O angels[17] sweet and splendid,
Throng in our hearts[18] and sing
The wonders that attended
The coming[19] of the King;
Till we,[20] too, boldly pressing,[21]
Where once[22] the shepherds[23] trod,
Climb[24] Bethlehem's Hill of Blessing
And find the Son[25] of God.

17. Both hands sweep up and out. 18. Hands move down and meet at the breast. 19. Left hand remains at the breast while the right hand moves slowly out to the side. 20. Both hands meet at the breast. 21. Holding former position, take two steps forward firmly. 22. Lift head with expression of wonder. 23. Right hand moves slowly out to side; gaze follows. 24. Right hand moves upward with gaze following. 25. Hands are crossed at the breast and head is flung back with expression of great joy.

———●◆●———

Recitation

A CHRISTMAS THOUGHT

There's going to come a time, we know,
When Christmas day will be gone
With only the memory of candle glow
And shouts of the happy dawn.

But we may keep ever within our hearts
Its message so dear and blest
And to others each day its joy impart
As we shelter the Christmas Guest.

HEAR THE CHRISTMAS BELLS.

(This Chorus may be rendered by a group of Children not used in the Cantata or by the Group of Young People. They may each carry a large red paper bell which they sway in time to the music each time the chorus is sung.)

MATTIE B. SHANNON.   CAROLYN R. FREEMAN.

1. Hear the Christmas bells now ring-ing,   Send-ing out a cheer-y song;
2. Hear the Christmas bells now chim-ing,   Clear-toned echoes float a - far;
3. Hear the Christmas bells now peal-ing,   Glad-ly lis-ten as they swing;

Joy a-round the world is wing-ing   To a wait-ing throng.
Could there be a sweet - er rhym-ing   'Neath the Christ-mas star?
Ev - 'ry note is joy re - veal-ing   As they gai-ly ring.

CHORUS.

"Mer - ry, mer - ry Christ - mas," Can you hear them chime? Ring-ing joy and glad - ness At the Christ-mas time; Borne on chant-ing breez - es, Wing-ing far a - way, Bells now sound a hap - py greet-ing For the Christmas Day.

Copyright, 1931, by Stockton Press.

'TIS LOVE MAKES OUR CHRISTMAS SO DEAR.

MATTIE B. SHANNON.   CAROLYN R. FREEMAN.

1. We pause in the midst of the Christ-mas- tide mirth And list to a
2. The Christ of the man - ger shall o - pen each heart, To those who a -

mes - sage of cheer,—..... We know, thro' the bless-ing of Je - sus to
wait He draws near;........ And this is the mes- sage our lips would im -

CHORUS.

earth, 'Tis love makes our Christmas so dear.........}
part, 'Tis love makes our Christmas so dear.........} Sweet is the mes-sage now

ring - ing, Lis - ten -ing hearts ev - er hear,.......... Shown in our

serv -ice to oth - ers, 'Tis love makes our Christmas so dear................

CHRISTMAS CHIMES

BARBARA STUART

C. HAROLD LOWDEN

1. Hap - py chimes a - gain are ring - ing;—
2. Bless - ed chimes pro-claim the sea - son

Joy - ous notes of Christ-mas - tide; In their songs a mes - sage wing - ing
Loved by old as well as young; Love - ly car - ols tell the rea - son,—

That will ev - er - more a - bide. From each stee - ple comes a cho - rus;—
Ring - ing out from ev - 'ry tongue; "Spend the time in thought for oth - ers,"

'Tis a mer - ry, mer - ry lay; In the mu - sic sound - ing o'er us ,
This the Christ-mas chimes would say; "Keep-ing true, a - bove all oth - ers,

Is the joy of Christ-mas Day. Bless-ed chimes a-gain are ring-ing; Hap-py voi - ces,
Hap - py,hap - py Christ-mas Day!"

too, are sing - ing; Mer - ri - ly they seem to say, "Come! Re-joice for Christ-mas Day!"